The Way to Wealth

or Poor Richard's Maxims Improved

to which is added

The Whistle
A True Story

&

The Advantages
of Drunkenness

Benjamin Franklin

Juniper Grove

Editor's Note

Though written more than 200 years ago, *The Way to Wealth* contains many timeless adages and bits of wisdom that are still incredibly applicable to our lives today. This edition has been compiled and edited from multiple early copies of *The Way to Wealth* and *The Whistle*, as well as the original editions of several of Poor Richard's Almanacks. A few words have been replaced with their more modern counterparts; as an example, the antiquated "bye-paths" was changed to "bypaths." Some of the more archaic or arcane words have been defined in footnotes.

J.L. Pope

ISBN 978-1-60355-100-7

Contents

The Way to Wealth

From 1732 to 1758, Benjamin Franklin wrote the highly successful *Poor Richard's Almanack* under the pseudonym "Richard Saunders." In *The Way to Wealth*, Franklin is again writing as Saunders, who stops at an auction and listens to a speech given by a character named Father Abraham. Phrases that originally appeared in *Poor Richard's Almanack* are italicized within the text.

Courteous Reader,

I have heard that nothing gives an author so great pleasure as to find his works respectfully quoted by other learned authors. This pleasure I have seldom enjoyed; for though I have been, if I may say it without vanity, an eminent author (of Almanacks) annually, now a full quarter of a century, my brother authors in the same way (for what reason I know not,) have ever been very sparing in their applauses; and no other author has taken the least notice of me; so that, did not my writings produce me some solid pudding[1], the great deficiency of praise would have quite discouraged me.

I concluded at length that the people were the best judges of my merit, for they buy my works; and besides, in my rambles, where I am not personally known, I have frequently heard one or other of my adages repeated with

1 provide a means of living; put food on the table

at the end on't. This gave me some satisfaction; as it showed not only that my instructions were regarded, but discovered likewise some respect for my authority; and I own, that, to encourage the practice of remembering and repeating those wise sentences, I have sometimes quoted myself with great gravity.

Judge, then, how much I must have been gratified by an incident I am going to relate to you. I stopped my horse lately where a great number of people were collected at an Auction of Merchant Goods. The hour of sale not being come, they were conversing on the badness of the times, and one of the company called to a plain, clean old man, with white locks. "Pray, Father Abraham, what think you of the times? Won't these heavy taxes quite ruin the country? How shall we be ever able to pay them? What would you advise us to do?"

Father Abraham stood up and replied — "If you'd have my advice, I'll give it to you in short: for *a word to the wise is enough*; and *many words won't fill a bushel*, as Poor Richard says." They joined in desiring him to speak his mind; and gathering round him, he proceeded as follows:

"Friends (says he) and neighbors, the taxes are indeed very heavy; and if those laid on by the government were the only ones we had to pay, we might more easily discharge them; but we have many others and much more grievous to some of us. We are taxed twice as much by our idleness, three times as much by our pride, and four times as much by our folly; and from these taxes the commissioner cannot ease or deliver us by allowing an abatement. However, let us hearken to good advice, and something may be done for us:

God helps them that help themselves,

as Poor Richard says in his Almanack.

It would be thought a hard government that should tax its people one-tenth part of their time, to be employed in its service: but idleness taxes many of us much more, if we reckon all that is spent in absolute sloth, or doing of nothing, with that which is spent in idle employments, or amusements that amount to nothing.

Sloth, by bringing on disease, absolutely shortens life. *Sloth, like rust, consumes faster than labour wears, while the key used is always bright*, as Poor Richard says.

But dost thou love life? then do not squander time, for *that's the stuff life is made of*, as Poor Richard says. How much more than is necessary do we spend in sleep! forgetting that *the sleeping fox catches no poultry*, and that *there will sleeping enough in the grave*, as Poor Richard says. *If time be of all things the most precious, wasting time must be* (as Poor Richard says) *the greatest prodigality*[2]; since, as he elsewhere tells us, *Lost time is never found again*; and *what we call time enough always proves little enough*.

---

2 imprudence; waste

Let us then up and be doing, and doing to the purpose; so by diligence shall we do more with less perplexity. *Sloth makes all things difficult, but industry all easy*, as Poor Richard says; and, *he that riseth late must trot all day, and shall scarce overtake his business at night*; while *laziness travels so slowly that poverty soon overtakes him*, as we read in Poor Richard, who adds, *Drive thy business; let not that drive thee*, and

Early to bed, and early to rise,
Makes a man healthy, wealthy, and wise.

So what signifies wishing and hoping for better times? We make these times better if we bestir ourselves. *Industry needs not wish*, as Poor Richard says; and,

He that lives upon hope will die fasting.

There are no gains without pains; then *help, hands, for I have no lands*, or if I have, they are smartly taxed; and, (as Poor Richard likewise observes,) *He that hath a trade, hath an estate*; and *he that hath a calling, hath an office of profit and honour*; but then the trade must be worked at, and the calling well followed, or neither the estate nor the office will enable us to pay our taxes.

If we are industrious, we shall never starve; for, as Poor Richard says, *At the working man's house hunger looks in, but dares not enter.* Nor will the bailiff or the constable enter; for *Industry pays debts, while despair increaseth them,* says Poor Richard. What though you have found no treasure, nor has any rich relation left you a legacy? *Diligence is the mother of good luck*, as Poor Richard says; and, *God gives all things to industry*;

Then plough deep while sluggards sleep,
And you will have corn to sell and to keep.

says Poor Dick.

Work while it is called today; for you know not how much you may be hindered tomorrow; which makes Poor Richard say, *One today is worth two tomorrows*, and further, *Have you somewhat to do tomorrow, do it today.* If you were a servant, would you not be ashamed that a good master should catch you idle? Are you then your own master? *Be ashamed to catch yourself idle*, as Poor Dick says.

When there is so much to be done for yourself, your family, your country, and your gracious king, be up by peep of day; *Let not the sun look down, and say, Inglorious here he lies!*

Handle your tools without mittens; remember that *the cat in gloves catches no mice*, as Poor Richard says. It is true, there is much to be done, and perhaps you are weak handed; but stick to it steadily, and you will see great effects; for, *constant dropping wears away stones*, and *by diligence and patience the mouse ate into the cable*; and *light strokes fell great oaks*, as Poor Richard says in his Almanack, the year I cannot just now remember.

Methinks I hear some of you say, "Must a man afford himself no leisure?" — I will tell thee, my friend, what Poor Richard says, *Employ thy time well if thou meanest to gain leisure*; and, *since thou art not sure of a minute, throw not away an hour.* Leisure is time for doing something useful; this leisure the diligent man will obtain, but the lazy man never; so that, as Poor Richard says, *A life of leisure and a life of laziness are two things.* Do you imagine that sloth will afford you more comfort than labour? No, for as Poor Richard says, *Trouble springs from Idleness, and grievous toil form endless ease. Many, without labour, would live by their wits only, but they break for want of stock*; whereas industry gives comfort, and plenty, and respect. *Fly*[3] *pleasures, and they will follow you. The diligent spinner has a large shift*; and *now I have a sheep and a cow, everybody bids me good morrow*; all which is well said by Poor Richard.

But with our industry, we must likewise be steady, settled, and careful, and oversee our own affairs with our own eyes, and not trust too much to others; for, as Poor Richard says,

> *I never saw an oft-removed tree,*
> *Nor yet an oft-removed family,*
> *That throve so well as those that settled be.*

And again, *Three removes is as bad as a fire*; and again, *Keep thy shop, and thy shop will keep thee*; and again, *if you would have your business done, go; if not, send.* And again,

---

3 flee from

He that by the plough would thrive,
Himself must either hold or drive.

And again, *the eye of a master will do more work than both his hands*; and again, *Want of care does us more damage than want of knowledge*; and again, *Not to oversee workmen, is to leave them your purse open.*

Trusting too much to others care is the ruin of many; for, *In the affairs of this world, men are saved, not by faith, but by the want of it*; but a man's own care is profitable; for, sayeth Poor Dick, *Learning is to the studious, and riches to the careful, as well as power to the bold, and heaven to the virtuous.* And farther, *If you would have a faithful servant, and one that you like, serve yourself.* And again, he adviseth to circumspection and care, even in the smallest matters, because sometimes a little neglect may breed great mischief. *For want of a nail the shoe was lost; for want of a shoe the horse was lost; and for want of a horse the rider was lost*; being overtaken and slain by the enemy, all for want of care about a horseshoe nail.

So much for industry, my friends, and attention to one's own business; but to these we must add frugality, if we would make our industry more certainly successful.

A man may, if he knows not how to save as he gets, *keep his nose all his life to the grindstone, and die not worth a groat*[4] *at last. A fat kitchen makes a lean will*, as Poor Richard says; and,

---

4 a coin of little value; a penny

Many estates are spent in the getting;
Since women for tea forsook spinning and knitting,
And men for punch[5] *forsook hewing and splitting.*

If you would be wealthy, (says he, in another Almanack,) *think of saving, as well as of getting: The Indies have not made Spain rich, because her outgoes are greater than her incomes.*

Away, then, with your expensive follies, and you will not have much cause to complain of hard times, heavy taxes, and chargeable families; for, as Poor Dick says,

Women and wine, game and deceit,
Make the wealth small, and the wants great.

And further, *What maintains one vice would bring up two children.* You may think, perhaps, that a little punch, now and then, diet a little more costly, clothes a little finer, and a little entertainment now and then, can be no great matter; but remember what Poor Richard says, *Many a little makes a mickle*[6]; and further, *Beware of little expenses; a small leak will sink a great ship*; and again, *Who dainties love, shall beggars prove*; and moreover,

Fools make feasts, and wise men eat them.

Here you are all got together at this sale of fineries and knickknacks. You call them GOODS; but, if you do not

5 alcohol
6 a lot; a large amount

take care, they will prove EVILS to some of you. You expect they will be sold cheap, and perhaps they may, for less than they cost; but, if you have no occasion for them, they must be dear to you. Remember what Poor Richard says, *Buy what thou hast no need of, and ere*[7] *long thou shalt sell thy necessaries.* And again, *At a great pennyworth, pause a while.* He means, that perhaps the cheapness is apparent only, but not real; or the bargain, by straitening[8] thee in thy business, may do thee more harm than good. For in another place he says,

Many have been ruined by buying good pennyworths.

Again, Poor Richard says, *It is foolish to lay out money in a purchase of repentance*; and yet this folly is practiced every day at auctions, for want of minding the Almanack. *Wise men* (as Poor Dick says) *learn by others harms, fools scarcely by their own.* Many a one, for the sake of finery on the back, have gone with a hungry belly and half-starved their families.

Silk and satins, scarlet and velvets, (as Poor Richard says) *put out the kitchen fire.* These are not the necessaries of life, they can scarcely be called the conveniencies; and yet, only because they look pretty, how many want to have them? The artificial wants of mankind thus become more numerous than the natural: and, as Poor Richard says, *For one poor person there are a hundred indigent.*

By these and other extravagancies, the genteel are

---

7 before
8 bringing restriction, hardship, poverty

reduced to poverty, and forced to borrow of those whom they formerly despised, but who, through industry and frugality, have maintained their standing; in which case it appears plainly, that *a ploughman on his legs is higher than a gentleman on his knees*, as Poor Richard says. Perhaps they have had a small estate left them, which they knew not the getting of; they think *it is day, and will never be night*; that a little to be spent out of so much is not worth minding: *A child and a fool* (as Poor Richard says) *imagine twenty shillings and twenty years can never be spent*; but *always taking out of the meal-tub, and never putting in, soon comes to the bottom*; then, as Poor Dick says, *When the well is dry, they know the worth of water.* But this they might have known before, if they had taken his advice.

If you would know the value of money, *go and try to borrow some*; for *he that goes a borrowing, goes a sorrowing*, as Poor Richard says; and indeed so does he that lends to such people, when he goes to get it in again.

Poor Dick further advises, and says,

> *Fond pride of dress is sure a very curse,*
> *Ere fancy you consult, consult your purse.*

And again, *pride is as loud a beggar as want, and a great deal more saucy*[9]. When you have bought one fine thing, you must buy ten more, that your appearance may be all of a piece; but Poor Dick says, *it is easier to suppress the first desire than to satisfy all that follow it*; and it is as truly

---

9 disrespectful

folly for the poor to ape the rich, as the frog to swell, in order to equal the ox.

Vessels large may venture more,
But little boats should keep near shore.

'Tis, however, a folly soon punished; for *Pride that dines on vanity, sups on contempt*, as Poor Richard says. And in another place,

Pride breakfasted with Plenty,
Dined with Poverty,
And supped with Infamy.

And, after all, of what use is this pride of appearance, for which so much is risked, so much is suffered? It cannot promote health, nor ease pain; it makes no increase of merit in the person; it creates envy; it hastens misfortune.

What is a butterfly? at best
He's but a caterpillar drest;
The gaudy fop's[10] *his picture just,*

as Poor Richard says.

But what madness must it be to run in debt for these superfluities! We are offered by the terms of this sale six months credit; and that perhaps has induced some of us to attend it, because we cannot spare the ready money,

---

10 one who attempts to gain admiration by overdressing and acting superior to others

and hope now to be fine without it. But ah! think what you do when you run in debt; you give to another power over your liberty. If you cannot pay at the time, you will be ashamed to see your creditor, you will be in fear when you speak to him, you will make poor, pitiful, sneaking excuses, and, by degrees, come to lose your veracity, and sink into base, downright lying; for, as Poor Richard says, *the second vice is lying, the first is running in debt.*

And again, to the same purpose, *Lying rides upon debt's back*; whereas a free born Englishman ought not to be ashamed nor afraid to see or speak to any man living. But poverty often deprives a man of all spirit and virtue. *It is hard for an empty bag to stand upright*, as Poor Richard truly says.

What would you think of that prince, or of that government, who should issue an edict forbidding you to dress like a gentleman or gentlewoman, on pain of imprisonment or servitude? Would you not say, that you were free, have a right to dress as you please, and that such an edict would be a breach of your privileges, and such a government tyrannical? And yet you are about to put yourself under that tyranny, when you run into debt for such dress! Your creditor has authority, at his pleasure, to deprive you of your liberty, by confining you in jail for life, or by selling you for a servant, if you should not be able to pay him.

When you have got your bargain, you may, perhaps, think little of payment; but *Creditors* (Poor Richard tells us) *have better memories than debtors*; and, in another place, he says,

> *Creditors are a superstitious sect,*
> *great observers of set days and times.*

The day comes round before you are aware, and the demand is made before you are prepared to satisfy it; or, if you bear your debt in mind, the term which at first seemed so long, will, as it lessens, appear extremely short; time will seem to have added wings to his heels as well as his shoulders.

Those have a short Lent, (sayeth Poor Richard,) *who owe money to be paid at Easter.* Then since, as he says, *The borrower is a slave to the lender, and the debtor to the creditor*, disdain the chain, preserve your freedom, and maintain your independence;

> *Be industrious and free, be frugal and free.*

At present, perhaps, you may think yourselves in thriving circumstances, and that you can bear a little extravagance without injury; but

> *For age and want save what you may,*
> *No morning sun lasts a whole day,*

as Poor Richard says. *Gain may be temporary and uncertain; but, ever while you live, expense is constant and certain*; and *it is easier to build two chimneys, than to keep one in fuel*, as Poor Richard says. So, *rather go to bed supperless than rise in debt.*

Get what you can, and what you get hold,
'Tis the stone that will turn all your lead into gold,

as Poor Richard says. And when you have got the philosopher's stone, sure you will no longer complain of bad times, or the difficulty of paying taxes.

This doctrine, my friends, is reason and wisdom; but, after all, do not depend too much upon your own industry, and frugality, and prudence, though excellent things; for they may all be blasted, without the blessing of heaven; and therefore ask that blessing humbly, and be not uncharitable to those that at present seem to want it, but comfort and help them. Remember Job suffered, and was afterwards prosperous.

And now to conclude, *Experience keeps a dear school; but fools will learn in no other, and scarce in that*; for, it is true, *we may give advice, but we cannot give conduct*, as Poor Richard says. However, remember this, *They that will not be counselled, cannot be helped*; as Poor Richard says; and further, that

If you will not hear reason, she will rap your knuckles."

Thus the old gentleman ended his harangue. The people heard it, and approved the doctrine; and immediately practiced the contrary, just as if it had been a common sermon; for the auction opened, and they began to buy extravagantly, notwithstanding all his cautions, and their own fear of taxes.

I found the good man had thoroughly studied my Almanacks, and digested all I had dropt on those topics during the course of twenty-five years. The frequent mention he made of me must have tried anyone else; but my vanity was wonderfully delighted with it, though I was conscious that not a tenth part of the wisdom was my own, which he ascribed to me, but rather the gleanings that I had made of the sense of all ages and nations. However, I resolved to be the better for the echo of it; and, though I had at first determined to buy stuff for a new coat, I went away, resolved to wear my old one a little longer. Reader, if thou wilt do the same, thy profit will be as great as mine.

I am, as ever, thine to serve thee,
Richard Saunders.

The Whistle
A True Story

On November 10, 1779, Franklin penned this tale in a letter to his friend Madame Brillon. He was living in Passy, France at the time, working as the first American ambassador to France.

When I was a child at seven years old, my friends, on a holiday, filled my pockets with coppers. I went directly to a shop, where they sold toys for children; and being charmed with the sound of a whistle that I met by the way in the hands of another boy, I voluntary offered him all my money for it. I then came home, and went whistling all over the house, much pleased with my whistle, but disturbing all the family. My brothers and sisters, and cousins, understanding the bargain I had made, told me I had given four times as much for it as it was worth. This put me in mind what good things I might have bought with the rest of the money; and they laughed at me so much for my folly, that I cried with vexation; and the reflection gave me more chagrin than the whistle gave me pleasure.

This, however, was afterwards of use to me, the impression continuing on my mind; so that often when I was tempted to buy some unnecessary thing, I said to myself, *Don't give too much for the whistle*; and so I saved my money.

As I grew up, came into the world, and observed the actions of men, I thought I met with many, very many, who gave too much for the whistle.

When I saw anyone too ambitious of court favours, sacrificing his time in attendance on levées[11], his repose, his liberty, his virtue, and perhaps his friends, to attain it, I have said to myself, *This man gives too much for his whistle.*

When I saw another fond of popularity, constantly employing himself in political battles, neglecting his own affairs, and ruining them by that neglect; *He pays, indeed*, says I, *too much for his whistle.*

If I knew a miser, who gave up every kind of comfortable living, all the pleasure of doing good to others, all the esteem of his fellow citizens, and the joys of benevolent friendship, for the sake of accumulating wealth: *Poor man*, says I, *you do indeed pay too much for your whistle.*

When I meet a man of pleasure, sacrificing every laudable improvement of the mind, or of his fortune, to mere corporeal sensations: *Mistaken man*, says I, *you are providing pain for yourself instead of pleasure, you give too much for your whistle.*

If I see one fond of fine clothes, fine furniture, fine equipages, all above his fortune, for which he contracts debts, and ends his career in prison. *Alas!* says I, *he has*

---

11 royal receptions

paid dear, very dear, for his whistle.

When I see a beautiful, sweet-tempered girl married to an ill-natured husband; *What a pity it is*, says I, *that she has paid so much for a whistle!*

In short, I conceived that a great part of the miseries of mankind were brought upon them by the false estimates they had made of the value of things, and by their giving too much for their whistles.

The Advantages of Drunkenness

Oh! that man should put an enemy into their mouths to steal away their brains. Shakespeare

All the enemies on the earth do not destroy so many of the human race, nor alienate so much property as drunkenness. Lord Bacon

If you wish to be always thirsty, be a drunkard; for the oftener and more you drink, the oftener and more thirsty you will be.

If you seek to prevent your friends from raising you in the world, be a drunkard; for that will defeat all their efforts.

If you would effectually counteract your own attempts to do well, be a drunkard; and you will not be disappointed.

If you wish to repel the endeavours of the whole human race to raise you to character, credit, and prosperity, be a drunkard; and you will assuredly triumph.

If you are determined to be poor, be a drunkard; and you will soon be ragged and pennyless.

If you would wish to starve your family, be a drunkard;

for that will consume the means of their support.

If you would be sponged on by knaves, be a drunkard; and that will make their task easy.

If you wish to be robbed, be a drunkard; which will enable the thief to do it with more safety.

If you wish to blunt your senses, be a drunkard; and you will soon be more stupid than an ass.

If you would become a fool, be a drunkard; and you will soon lose your understanding.

If you wish to incapacitate yourself for rational intercourse, be a drunkard; for that will render you wholly unfit for it.

If you wish all your prospects in life to be clouded, be a drunkard; and they will be dark enough.

If you would destroy your body, be a drunkard; as drunkenness is the mother of disease.

If you mean to ruin your soul, be a drunkard; that you may be excluded from heaven.

If you are resolved on suicide, be a drunkard; that being a sure mode of destruction.

If you would expose both your folly and secrets, be a drunkard; and they will soon run out while the liquor runs in.

If you are plagued with great bodily strength, be a drunkard; and it will soon be subdued by so powerful an antagonist.

If you would get rid of your money without knowing how, be a drunkard; and it will vanish insensibly.

If you would have no other resource when past labour but a workhouse, be a drunkard; and you will be unable to provide any.

If you are determined to expel all domestic harmony from your house, be a drunkard; and discord, with all her train, will soon enter.

If you would be always under strong suspicion, be a drunkard; for, little as you think it, all agree that those who steal from themselves and families will rob others.

If you would be reduced to the necessity of shunning your creditors, be a drunkard; and you will soon have reason to prefer the bypaths to the public streets.

If you like the amusements of a court of conscience, be a drunkard; and you may be often gratified.

If you would be a dead weight to the community, and "cumber the ground," be a drunkard; for that will render you houseless, helpless, burdensome, and expensive.

If you would be a nuisance, be a drunkard; for the reproach of a drunkard is like that of a dunghill.

If you would be odious to your family and friends, be a drunkard; and you will soon be more than disagreeable.

If you would be a pest to society, be a drunkard; and you will be avoided as infectious.

If you dread reformation of your faults, be a drunkard; and you will be impervious to all admonition.

If you would smash windows, break the peace, get your bones broken, tumble under carts and horses, and be locked up in watch-houses, be a drunkard; and it will be strange if you do not succeed.

Finally, if you are determined to be utterly destroyed in estate, body, and soul, be a drunkard; and you will soon know that it is impossible to adopt a more effectual means to accomplish your — END.

Drunkenness expels reason — drowns the memory — defaces beauty — diminishes strength — inflames the blood — causes internal, external, and incurable wounds — is a witch to the senses, a devil to the soul, a thief to the purse — the beggar's companion, a wife's woe, and children's sorrow — makes a strong man weak, and a wise man a fool. He is worse than a beast, and is a self-murderer, who drinks to other's good health, and robs himself of his own.

Made in the USA
Monee, IL
06 June 2023

35364749R00016